The Renaissance
Science and Art Combined
Children's Renaissance history

BABY PROFESSOR

EDUCATION KIDS

Speedy Publishing LLC

40 E. Main St. #1156

Newark, DE 19711

www.speedypublishing.com

Copyright 2016

People's search to explore and expand their understanding of the world gave birth to the Renaissance. A new age of science started when people began to want to understand the world around them better.

In the Renaissance period, art and science were very closely related. To create better sculptures and paintings, artists like Leonardo da Vinci studied anatomy to better understand the body.

In order to design buildings, advances in math were made by architects like Filippo Brunelleschi. During that time, the true geniuses studied both science and artist.

DO YOU KNOW WHAT A RENAISSANCE MAN IS?

A man is considered a true Renaissance man when he has talents in many fields of arts and sciences.

M·FIL·SEVERO·P
O·PONTIFIC·
·ANTONINO
O·PTIMIS·F·C
STITVTAM
S·VIRTVTIB

ART AS EXPRESSIONS OF NEW IDEAS

To portray the new attitudes and ideas, artists in the Renaissance expressed their thoughts in their paintings and sculptures.

WHAT WERE NEW IDEAS AT THAT TIME?

There was a great focus and awareness on human abilities, needs, and interests. They called this humanism. Because of the new ideas, artists' choices of subject and the method of painting changed dramatically.

CHANGE OF SUBJECTS

Religion was the subject in almost all European art in the Middle Ages. The Catholic Church and Christianity were specifically portrayed.

Aside from religious subjects, they
also portrayed subjects like portraits
of individuals, historical subjects, and
Roman and Greek mythology. The details
of everyday life were the focus of artists.

THERE ARE TWO PERIODS IN RENAISSANCE ART:

- Early Renaissance from 1400 to 1479.

- High Renaissance from 1475 to 1525.

EARLY RENAISSANCE FROM 1400 TO 1479

The way that artists learned to do their work was by trying to imitate the work of classical artists. There was a great focus on making perfect forms and on symmetry. Artists such as Giotto, Masaccio, and Donatello were prominent in this era.

IS·AM BRO SI

HIGH RENAISSANCE FROM 1475 TO 1525

To give more realism to their work, there was a rise in the interest of understanding how to depict depth of space and perspective. During this period, Rafael, Leonardo da Vinci, and Michelangelo developed as great artists.

WHAT IS REALISM?

To sculpt and paint the subjects realistically was one of the biggest changes in art in those times. They called this realism. To make the background and subjects look how they would look in real life, a number of art techniques were involved. The aim was to give the subjects more emotional qualities by depicting them with rich accuracy.

WHAT WERE THE NEW STYLES AND TECHNIQUES?

Introduced during that time were many new techniques which helped in enhance the quality and realism of their artwork.

Use of Light and Dark - light and shadows were used by artists in their works to add an indication of time of day, and to show perspective and drama.

Balance and Proportion – the artist aimed to draw the subjects in their correct size as compared to each other.

MARKE

Perspective – this gives a three dimensional effect to the drawing or painting. The illusion is used to show that some objects are further away than the others in the painting.

Foreshortening - to give the illusion of depth, artists discovered foreshortening lines. This is another technique that added depth and perspective to the paintings.

Sfumato - to give additional dimension and perspective to paintings, Leonardo da Vinci used this technique. He used this in his great work, the Mona Lisa. To do this, the lines between the subjects are blurred.

REVOLUTION IN SCIENCE

The scientific revolution started near the end of the Renaissance. Great steps in science and mathematics happened. Discoveries that would change the world were done by scientists like Isaac Newton, Rene Descartes, Galileo, and Francis Bacon.

WHAT IS THE PRINTING PRESS?

In the history of the world, the printing press is considered one of the greatest inventions of the Renaissance. German Johannes Gutenberg invented this around 1440. The invention allowed information to be distributed quickly to many people. This also helped scientists share their discoveries and learn from each other. There were printing presses all over Europe by the 1500s.

DEVELOPED SCIENTIFIC METHOD

To prove or disprove his theories, Galileo used controlled experiments, gathered data, and analyzed the data. Isaac Newton and Francis Bacon later refined the process.

DISCOVERIES IN ASTRONOMY

Major contributions in this field were made by great scientists such as Kepler, Galileo, and Copernicus.

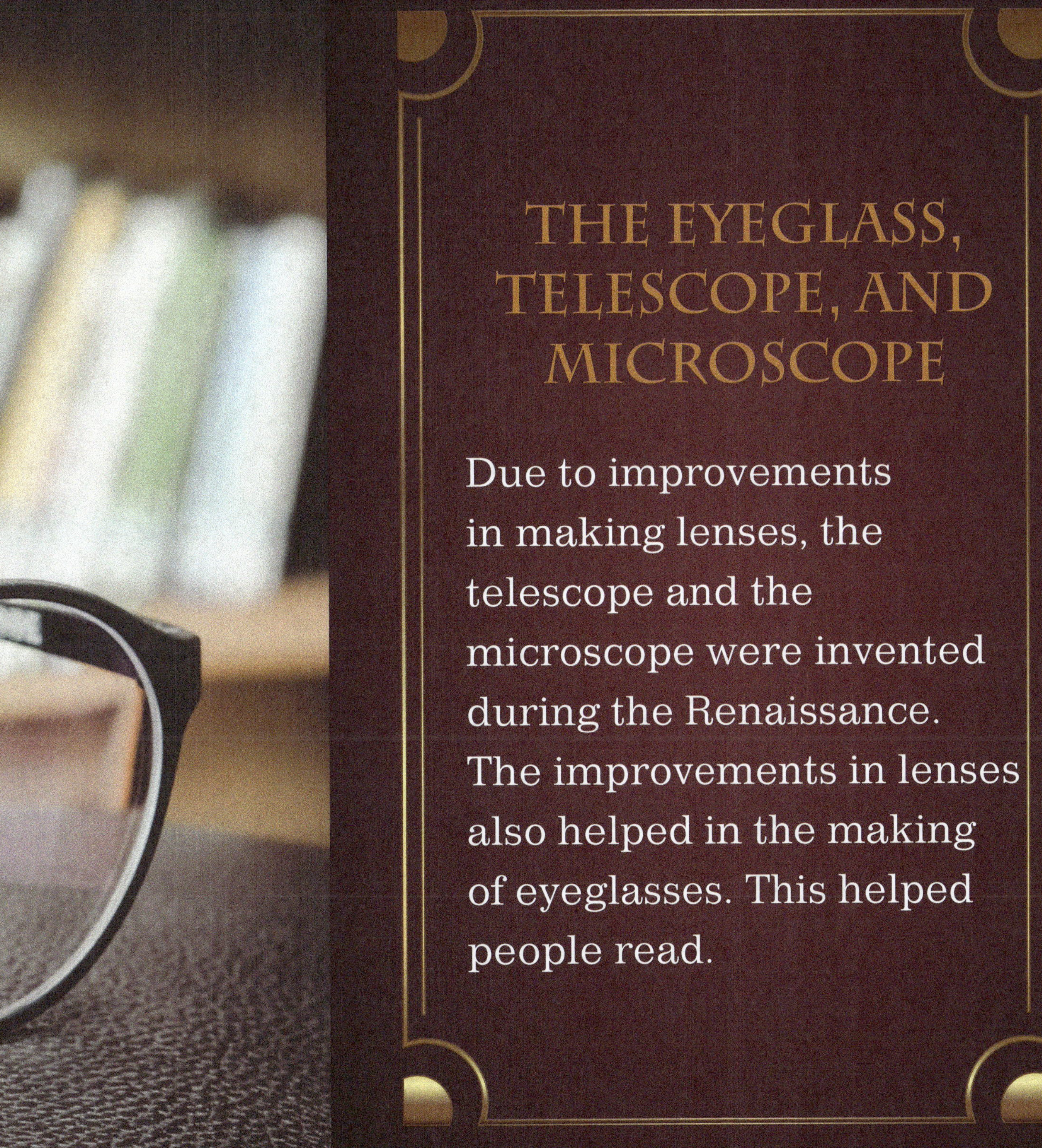

THE EYEGLASS, TELESCOPE, AND MICROSCOPE

Due to improvements in making lenses, the telescope and the microscope were invented during the Renaissance. The improvements in lenses also helped in the making of eyeglasses. This helped people read.

THE CLOCK

The pendulum was refined by Galileo in 1581. The invention of more accurate clocks was made possible by his work.

ADVANCEMENTS IN WARFARE

With the invention of weapons that fired metal balls using gunpowder, such as muskets and cannons, the dominance in wars of knights and castles ended.

WHAT ARE OTHER INVENTIONS DURING THE RENAISSANCE?

During those times, other inventions were the submarine, wallpaper, the screwdriver, the wrench, and the flush toilet.

Visit
BABY PROFESSOR
EDUCATION KIDS
www.BabyProfessorBooks.com
to download Free Baby Professor eBooks
and view our catalog of new and exciting
Children's Books

www.ingramcontent.com/pod-product-compliance
Lightning Source LLC
Chambersburg PA
CBHW060145120726
48003CB00009B/3033